KOMODO DRAGON

VS.

KING COBRA

BY
JERRY PALLOTTA

ILLUSTRATED BY
ROB BOLSTER

Scholastic Inc.

New York   Toronto   London   Auckland
Sydney   Mexico City   New Delhi   Hong Kong

The publisher would like to thank the following for their
kind permission to use their photographs in this book:

Page 16: © Jonathan and Angela Scott / NHPA / Photoshot; page 17: Animals Animals / SuperStoc
page 18: Skulls Unlimited International, Inc.; page 19: Skulls Unlimited International, Inc.;
page 20: Michael Pitts / Nature Picture Library; page 21: Gary Graham / Newspix / News Ltd.;
page 24: Andy Paradise / Rex USA; page 25: Blaine Harrington III / Corbis

Thank you to Dr. Stephen Durant, rugby player supreme!
—J.P.

Thank you to Mr. Winslow Homer.
—R.B.

ISBN 978-0-545-30171-8

57 56 55 54   24 25 26/0

Printed in the U.S.A.   40
First printing, Novermber 2011

What would happen if a tough Komodo dragon came face-to-face with a deadly king cobra? What if they were both hungry? If they had a fight, who do you think would win?

SCIENTIFIC NAME OF KOMODO DRAGON: "Varanus komodoensis"

Meet the Komodo dragon. The Komodo dragon is the largest lizard in the world. It grows up to ten feet long and can weigh three hundred pounds.

DEFINITION
A reptile is a cold-blooded animal covered in scales. Turtles, snakes, lizards, crocodiles, and alligators are reptiles.

FACT
Komodo dragons live on four Indonesian islands: Komodo, Rinca, Flores, and Gili Motang.

SCIENTIFIC NAME OF KING COBRA: "Ophiophagus hannah"

Meet the king cobra. A king cobra can grow up to eighteen feet long. The king cobra is a venomous snake that can weigh up to twenty pounds.

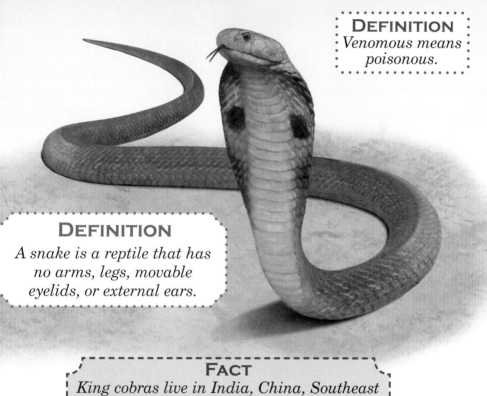

> **DEFINITION**
> *Venomous means poisonous.*

> **DEFINITION**
> *A snake is a reptile that has no arms, legs, movable eyelids, or external ears.*

> **FACT**
> *King cobras live in India, China, Southeast Asia, Indonesia, and the Philippines.*

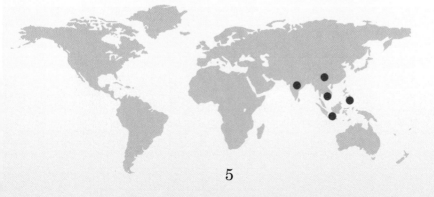

TEETH

Komodo dragons have teeth. Their teeth are unusual f̶
a land animal. They are serrated, like a shark's teeth.

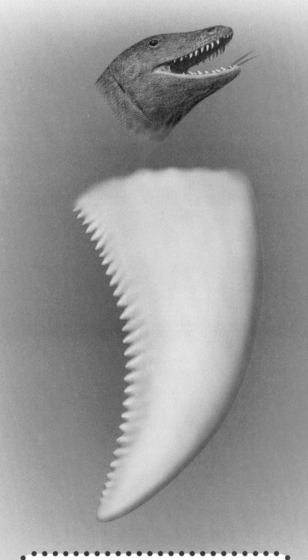

DANGEROUS FACT
Serrated means jagged, like a saw.

FANGS

King cobras have fangs. A fang is a long hollow tooth used to inject venom.

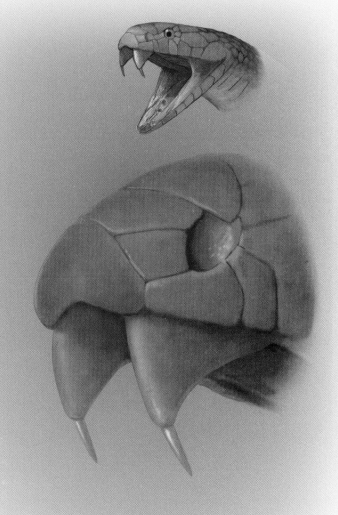

DEADLY

There are only three known poisonous lizards: the Gila monster, the Mexican beaded lizard, and the Komodo dragon. In addition to venom, the Komodo dragon has dangerous bacteria in its mouth.

> **DEFINITION**
> *A lizard is a reptile with two pairs of legs and a tail.*

GILA MONSTER

MEXICAN BEADED LIZARD

VENOM

A king cobra bite is deadly. A king cobra does not have the deadliest poison of all snakes. But it injects the most poison. Its poison is a neurotoxin. One king cobra bite has the strength to kill an elephant — or twenty people.

DANGEROUS DEFINITION

A neurotoxin is a poison that paralyzes its victim's nerves and muscles.

SNAKE TRIVIA

Some species of cobras can spit their venom, but a king cobra cannot.

FORKED

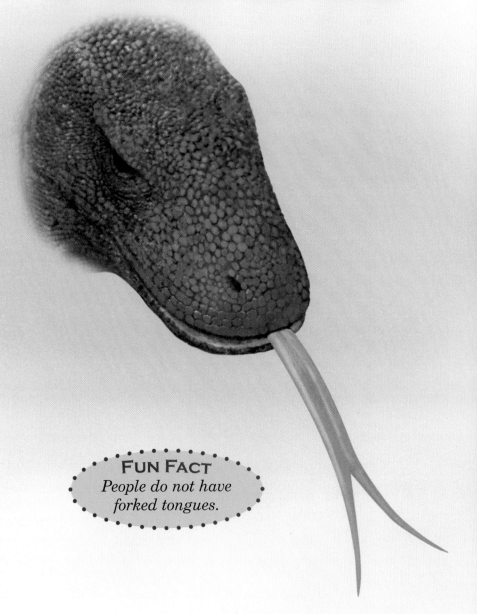

> **FUN FACT**
> *People do not have
> forked tongues.*

The Komodo dragon has a forked tongue. It splits into two
sides. A Komodo tongue is sensitive. When it flicks out its
tongue, it can detect where a deer might be nearby.

TONGUES

The king cobra also has a forked tongue. It smells with its tongue. Its tongue can also sense motion and temperature.

ABSOLUTE FACT

You do not want to get bitten by a king cobra!

S C A

The skin of a Komodo dragon looks like this.

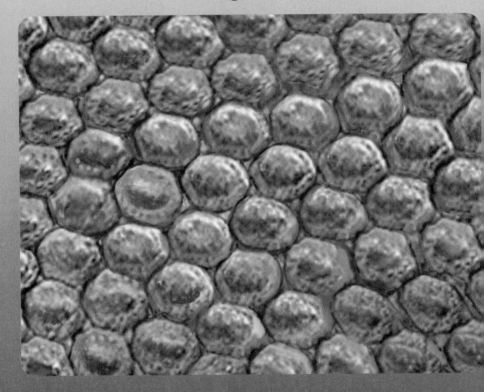

L E S

A king cobra is covered in scales. The scales are dry and not slimy. Most snakes' scales have a pattern.

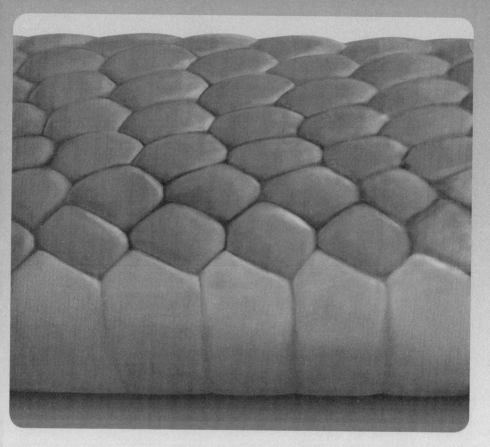

The skin of a king cobra looks like this. The belly scales are the widest.

> **INTERESTING FACT**
> *A group of cobras is called
> a quiver.*

KOMODO DRAGON SKULL

This is the skull of a Komodo dragon. It looks a bit flat, like the skulls of crocodiles and alligators.

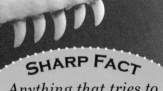

SHARP FACT

Anything that tries to escape it gets cut by the sharp side of its teeth.

WARNING!

You do NOT want to get bitten by a Komodo dragon.

OTHER KOMODO DRAGON NAMES

A Komodo dragon is also called an ora or a land crocodile.

KING COBRA SKULL

This is the skull of a king cobra. It does not have much of a skull. Its brain is mostly unprotected.

FUN FACT

The study of snakes is called ophiology or serpentology.

King cobras do not chew their food. In addition to fangs, they have small upper and lower teeth to pull food into their mouths. They swallow their prey whole.

QUESTION

Would you like to become a scientist and study snakes?

KOMODO DRAGON'S FAVORITE FOOD

Komodo dragons love to eat small mammals. They also eat lizards and snakes. They kill by tearing their prey to shreds.

GROSS FACT
Komodo dragons can easily eat half of their body weight.

DID YOU KNOW?
A Komodo dragon's venom prevents blood clotting. Its victims sometimes bleed to death.

DISGUSTING FACT
If a Komodo dragon eats too much hair, bones, nails, and scales, it coughs up a giant pellet.

KING COBRA'S FAVORITE FOOD

Snakes are the favorite food of king cobras. Their scientific name means "snake-eater."

JUST ATE

ONE MONTH

TWO MONTHS

FUN FACT
After eating a large meal, a king cobra might not eat again for one or two months.

WITH LEGS

Look at the skeletons of the Komodo dragon and king cobra. What differences do you notice right away?

VALUABLE FACT

The government of Indonesia minted a gold coin in honor of the Komodo dragon.

The Komodo dragon has legs and toes. It also has a distinct tail.

WITHOUT LEGS

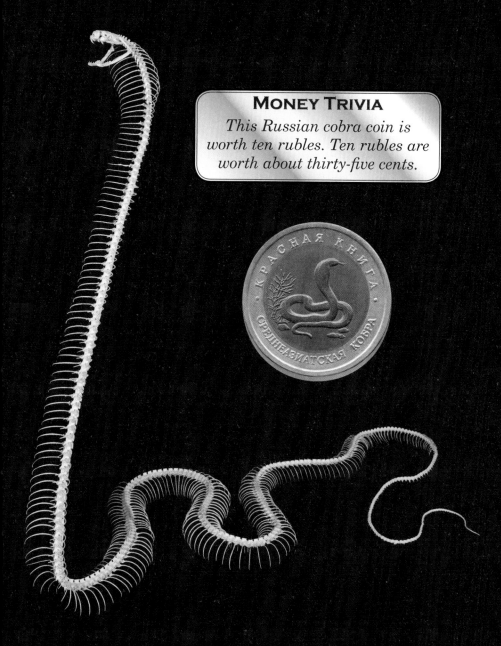

The king cobra has no legs, fingers, or toes. It has many ribs, making its body look like one long tail.

NEWLY

Mother Komodo dragons lay about twenty-five eggs per clutch. Komodo dragon babies live in trees. They eat bugs, small lizards, rodents, and eggs.

DEFINITION
A clutch is a group of eggs laid by birds or reptiles.

GROSS FACT
Young Komodo dragons roll in animal waste to protect themselves.

BORN

FUN FACT

As soon as they are born, baby king cobras have poisonous venom.

Here is a king cobra baby. A king cobra is the only snake that makes a nest. It looks like a bird's nest.

KING COBRA TRIVIA

After making a nest, mother king cobras lay between twenty and fifty eggs at a time.

STRANGE BEHAVIOR

DID YOU KNOW?
*Baby Komodo dragons are born
with stripes that disappear when
they grow up.*

A Komodo dragon sometimes eats its own children.
Young Komodos are smart enough to escape up a tree.

MORE STRANGE BEHAVIOR

A king cobra can spread its rib bones and make itself appear larger. This behavior is called making a hood.

HOOD!

NO HOOD!

> **FUN FACT**
>
> *The design on the back of this king cobra's head are called spectacle markings.*

ZOO

You can see a Komodo dragon in some zoos. The experienc
can be disappointing, because reptiles spend many hours
never moving.

INTERESTING FACT
*The branch of zoology that
studies reptiles is called
herpetology.*

QUESTION
*Would you like to become a
herpetologist?*

PETS

If you travel to India or Thailand, you might see a street performer doing tricks with a cobra.

FUN FACT
Some people have king cobras and other snakes for pets.

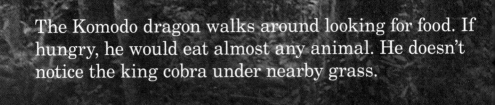

The Komodo dragon walks around looking for food. If hungry, he would eat almost any animal. He doesn't notice the king cobra under nearby grass.

INTERESTING FACT

Of all the animals on Earth, the Komodo dragon probably most resembles the look and walk of a dinosaur.

he cobra has no interest in the Komodo dragon. Snakes
ke to eat things they can swallow whole. The Komodo
ragon is way too big!

The Komodo dragon wanders a bit too close. The cobra raises its head, spreads its hood, and makes a growling sound. It is a warning to back off!

The cobra just wants to be left alone. The Komodo dragon circles around some more.

YIKES!
Not only can the king cobra slither on the ground, it can also swim and climb trees.

The clumsy Komodo dragon steps on the cobra's eggs by accident. The cobra strikes fast, biting the leg of the intruder! As soon as the cobra's fangs sink into the Komodo dragon's leg, they unload their venom.

The Komodo dragon walks a few steps, then starts to breathe heavily. Its legs get wobbly. It can't see, gets dizzy, and falls over.

The king cobra has killed the Komodo dragon with one deadly bite! Maybe next time, the Komodo dragon will bite first.

WHO HAS THE ADVANTAGE? CHECKLIST

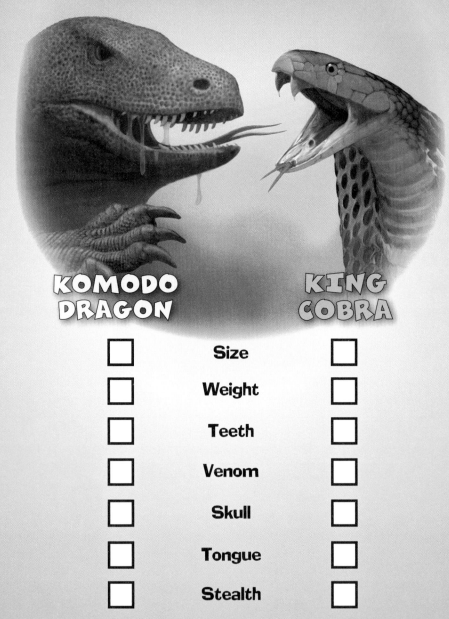

KOMODO DRAGON

KING COBRA

☐	Size	☐
☐	Weight	☐
☐	Teeth	☐
☐	Venom	☐
☐	Skull	☐
☐	Tongue	☐
☐	Stealth	☐

Author note: This is one way the fight might have ended. How would you write the ending?